Elizabeth's journey

accompanied by:

Andrews McMeel Publishing
a division of Andrews McMeel Universal
1130 Walnut Street, Kansas City, Missouri 64106

www.andrewsmcmeel.com

Picture Credits:
Labyrinth on p. 17: shutterstock.com
Titles of nobility on p. 119, image "House of Lords 1808": picture
alliance/Heritage Art/Heritage Images, J. Bluck

23 24 25 26 27 POA 10 9 8 7 6 5 4 3 2 1

ISBN: 978-1-5248-7688-3

Library of Congress Control Number: 2022944591

ATTENTION: SCHOOLS AND BUSINESSES
Andrews McMeel books are available at quantity discounts with
bulk purchase for educational, business, or sales promotional use.
For information, please e-mail the Andrews McMeel Publishing
Special Sales Department: sales@amuniversal.com.

FSC
www.fsc.org
MIX
Paper from
responsible sources
FSC® C136333

Hallet & Davis

Marjolein Bastin

The
Jane Austen
Escape Room
Book

Andrews McMeel
PUBLISHING®

Dear Readers,

The escape room book that you're holding in your hands might be a little different from anything you've seen before. The story of our main character, Elizabeth Bennet, doesn't take place in a closed room from which she has to escape. Instead, the young woman's task is to defy society's deep-rooted prejudices and flee its expectations. Despite the occurrence of a scandalous incident, will she be able to win back the heart of the noble and wealthy gentleman Mr. Darcy, or will this delicate situation result in her utter ruin? Find out here. Join us in England in the early 19th century, where our story begins in a stagecoach in the middle of nowhere ...

Introduction

Peony: courage

Before you join Miss Bennet on her journey, allow us to give you a few instructions. To play the game, you'll need not only your intuition but also all your social acumen.

Read each text carefully from start to finish and examine each page thoroughly—there might be something that will be useful to you later on. It won't hurt to review some passages and refresh your memory about what has gone on before.

Unfortunately, you're not allowed to look into the future and read subsequent pages ahead of time. If pages in the appendix are necessary for solving a puzzle, you'll find a corresponding note next to the puzzle itself ("Puzzle supplement XY"). Also in the appendix, you'll find your own personal notes pages for writing down thoughts, clues, and solutions. **You'll also need a pencil, scissors, and tape.** And because—as we all know—a lot of important things can be learned from the newspaper, a closer examination of what's in the appendix might provide you with some valuable insights if you're ever in need. Pay attention to the relevant box numbers. If you're absolutely desperate, you can find the answers to the puzzles at the end of the book. Now, join Elizabeth on her journey, and help her uncover all the intrigues, overcome the challenges, and win back Mr. Darcy's heart.

Dead-nettle: "I don't want to hear it."

Puzzle No. 1

The Stagecoach

Elizabeth is jostled awake by her seatmate on her left. Dazed, she opens her eyes. Sheep and trees pass before her in the dusk. Where is she? Where is her friend Charlotte, with whom she had just been dancing happily at the ball? What in the world happened?

The woman sitting across from her in the rocking coach doesn't seem to have noticed that Elizabeth is now awake. Still completely confused, Elizabeth struggles to order her thoughts and overhears the woman whisper to her neighbor, "... and it doesn't even seem to bother her that her charming and gallant companion left the coach at the last station. I've never seen anything like it." Her neighbor responds in a half whisper, "You're right; he was extremely charming and

8

gentlemanly. But didn't you think it was also strange and disturbing that he left the coach without her? A woman traveling alone in a stagecoach! It's scandalous! When we arrive, I'll have to tell Mrs. Nosy. Won't she be surp—" When they suddenly notice that Elizabeth is awake, they fall silent for a moment and then turn to more innocuous subjects.

"It's really extraordinarily good of your brother-in-law to invite us," says the woman directly across from Elizabeth. Elizabeth's seatmate who boarded more recently concurs. The third passenger answers, "Not at all; for him, it goes without saying! When I wrote and told him how long we were planning on staying, he asked why we didn't just remain for the whole 10 weeks. You'll see; it's truly delightful there. Not far from the border, so we're sure to be able to spend a few days at one of the lochs. The last time I visited, I stopped at the *Hamstead Inn*. The food there is heavenly, especially the specialty of the house, ham. You'll have to try it!" Elizabeth's seatmate says, "I can hardly wait," and the third passenger responds, "I'm so happy that you were able to accompany us on this trip, my dear. Since you moved north, we see much too little of each other." Elizabeth's seatmate smiles. "You calling it 'north' always amuses me." "Well, yes, it's north of us . . ." answers the other woman, embarrassed. "But it's still the south!" laughs Elizabeth's seatmate.

Elizabeth's head is still spinning. She looks out the window at the dusk and reflects. In the distance, she sees the arms of a windmill, a small church, a dark forest . . . no doubt a wonderful area. If she only knew how she ended up in this stagecoach and where she was headed. She doesn't dare ask her fellow passengers after hearing their disparaging words. Can she find out where the stagecoach is headed without help?

Puzzle No. 2

The Garden Maze

Gretna Green! In a flash, she realizes that that's where the stagecoach must be headed, the Mecca for all those intending to get married! The place where even men and women who are not of legal age can marry without their parents' consent. There's no telling what would happen if her family found out, let alone the neighborhood gossips and, above all, Mr. Darcy! Elizabeth shudders at the thought. Yes, she had long considered him arrogant, proud, and snobbish, but since his offer of marriage when she visited Hunsford, and since his letter, things have changed. She's certainly no longer indifferent to him . . . If she'd only had the courage to speak to him at the ball, but she was too confused by the latest developments and didn't know how she should behave around him. And now this! Elizabeth Bennet in a coach to Gretna Green with an unknown man.

If Mr. Darcy ever came to hear about this scandalous event, he would certainly avoid any contact with her in the future and lose all interest. Elizabeth's heart grows heavy.

She hears the woman across from her say, "Thank goodness we can finally leave this horrible coach! When we continue tomorrow, I'll wear lighter clothing. Let's go to my brother immediately. He lives near London Bridge." Relieved, Elizabeth exits the stagecoach with the other passengers. She decides that her first move should be to seek refuge with her uncle and aunt, Mr. and Mrs. Gardiner, who live in London. On the way to their home, she tries again and again to remember how she came to be in the coach, but to no avail. Was she unconscious? Tired out, she finally reaches her uncle's property. Beyond the labyrinthine garden, she recognizes the house in the misty darkness.

Oh no, bad luck! It seems that her aunt and uncle weren't expecting any more visitors at this late hour and have extinguished all the lanterns in the garden. She struggles to make out the path directly in front of her in the weak moonlight. **She remembers the general outline but won't be able to see any obstacles in this darkness.** In her last letter, her aunt told her about a mole that had wreaked havoc right at the entrance to the circle and had driven the gardener to distraction. With her tall, elegant dancing shoes, she won't be able to get through this way, and she doesn't want to add broken bones to everything else that's happened. So she can't take the direct route. With a sigh, she takes the path heading north. But what's that? She suddenly feels water seeping into her flimsy shoes, and it gets deeper with each step. The heavy rainfall over the past few days must have left behind enormous puddles.

Without having achieved anything, she turns around. Before starting up again, she tries to remember exactly what her aunt wrote. Elizabeth seems to recall her aunt mentioning that the eastern entrance by the large fountain in the center of the garden was currently closed due to maintenance work on the fountain. A southeastern passage near the house was unfortunately completely overgrown, and the hedge was in desperate need of pruning. Will she ever get there?

Ivy: dependability and faithfulness, immortality

Violet: honesty, humility, respectability, paradise, spring, and hope

Puzzle No. 3

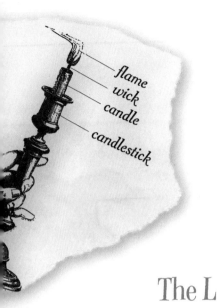

flame
wick
candle
candlestick

The Letter from Charlotte

When she finally reaches the Gardiners' house and enters, her relatives are astonished. "Lizzy! What are you doing here at such a late hour? We didn't expect you until tomorrow. We thought you wanted to stop off here with us in London on your way back from your friend Charlotte's! Has something happened to make you cut short your visit to the Collins family?" Agitated, Elizabeth tells them about the evening's events.

"What should I do? My family will be beside themselves when they find out. The news will spread like wildfire. Everyone will think that I secretly ran away with this man. My poor mother and her poor nerves . . ." "Dearest, remain with us for now," says Mrs. Gardiner. Elizabeth gratefully accepts her offer.

While they're all trying to work out what happened, Elizabeth finds a note from her friend Charlotte in her pocket. She reads it aloud: "Dear Lizzy, here are the dance steps for later on, so you'll know how and **where** you have to go and won't fall out of step with the dance. Love, Charlotte."

"Strange," says Elizabeth. "Why would Charlotte hand me instructions like these when she knows that I know the steps of every dance by heart?! And is that supposed to be the Country Dance? . . ." She examines the note more closely.

Yellow tulip: one-sided love

Bluebottle: "I won't lose hope."

Puzzle
supplement

The
Country Dance

Pink tulips: tender, burgeoning love

Puzzle No. 4

Gentian: faithfulness but also magnificent beauty

The Find

The next day, Elizabeth excitedly makes her way to Charlotte's suggested meeting place, St. Paul's Cathedral. What is her mysterious message about? Just as she turns the corner, the clock strikes 2:00 and she sees a relieved Charlotte rushing toward her. "Lizzy! Thank goodness! What happened? Where have you been? I'm so glad you're all right. When you suddenly disappeared from the ball, I feared the worst." Elizabeth answers, "Charlotte, I'm so happy to see you. But I can't tell you what happened; I don't understand it, either. I remember that after several dances, I went outside to get some air and refresh myself with a drink." "Yes, I guessed all that," says Charlotte. "That's why I followed you there, but I couldn't find a trace. I then asked around and found out that you'd disappeared from the terrace in the company of a young man. They even said that he'd put his arm around you in an intimate embrace and that you left the ball in one another's arms. Rumor had it that your destination was the stagecoach to Gretna Green. At least that's what Lady Hearsay supposedly heard your companion say, who was raving to her about you. Lizzy, what does it all mean? It isn't true, is it? Today, there was even something about it in the newspaper! But I just don't believe it." "Good gracious!" Elizabeth responds. "None of that is true. Except that I really did wake up in a coach to Gretna Green. I just can't remember how I got there."

Elizabeth's head is swimming. Her worst fears have been confirmed. She tries hard to remember. The last thing she can recall is the face of a servant who personally placed a drink in her hand. A specialty of the house, he had said. Something absolutely exquisite. What was it called? A laudatini? But she can't remember any young man.

As she looks at her friend's sympathetic face, she suddenly remembers the mysterious message. "Why exactly did you want to meet me?" Elizabeth asks. Charlotte answers, "I found this strange piece of paper at the ball and couldn't make heads or tails of it. I hoped I could speak to you alone and in confidence, so I slipped you my message at the ball while you were in conversation with someone else. I knew that you wanted to leave for your uncle's in London early Sunday morning and I wouldn't have an opportunity to speak to you beforehand because of a visit to our neighbor Lady Catherine de Bourgh that was arranged far in advance. Since I was going to be in London today in any case, I thought it would be a good opportunity to talk about my strange find."

Together, the two friends look down at the piece of paper that had apparently been crumpled up and carelessly discarded. "What do the numbers mean?" Charlotte asks. "If only my husband, Mr. Collins, were here! He's splendid with numbers. A1, as he likes to say. It's just one of his qualities, as he humbly admits." They both look back at the paper and are convinced that it can bring them one step closer to solving the mystery.

Crocus: "Give me time to think it over."

$(A = 1/2 = 2/6 = 3/9 = 4..)$

14 15 9 3 18 17 14 13 16 15
25 12 16 9 12 25
23 13 3 18 1 18 4

Tin Plates,

FOR SALE BY

WALKER,

Pine, near Fifth Street.

1W

SIMON WALKER,

A House in Burlington for Sale.

December 8

THE subscriber has a large, convenient two-
brick House, with Stables, Carriage-
a well improved Garden, in the City of
-Jersey which he wishes to SELL.
No. South Fourth Street, to

for Sale,
City,
principal

Imported (via New York) on the

Ship Hero, from Madras and Calcutta, and for
sale by the subscriber, at No. 61, Chestnut Street,
between Second and Third Streets, the following
articles.

Mabaragonges
Chintz and Calicoes
Gillis Romals
Nillas & Pensiasoes
Blue cloth
Mull Mullhankerchiefs
Patna   do.
Lesser Cardimum
Seeds.

Charconna Dorens
Dacca worked muslins
Bandannoes
Chasla Romals
Hair ribbon
Palempores
Banares Opium

Samuel Wilcox

November 27.

To Gentlemen who intend Spending the Winter in the City

ROOMS to LET,

WITH or without Board—at No. 14 corner of
and Race Streets. The situation agree-
nity has been free from the late

Oct. 27—dtf

TICE.

ENLEAF's

ments

ted.

Lavender: faithfulness

Puzzle No. 5

White lily: pure love, innocence, also death.

The Librarian

After Charlotte and Elizabeth solve the puzzle of the mysterious note, they say goodbye to one another. Charlotte completes her errands in London, and she and her servants return to Hunsford so as not to keep her husband waiting. Elizabeth makes her way back to her aunt and uncle. When she tells them about her strange discovery, her uncle declares that he's ready to accompany her.

The next day, Elizabeth and Mr. Gardiner enter the grand hall of the venerable British Museum Library. But what now? Maybe the scowling librarian can help them. While her uncle talks to him, Elizabeth lets her eyes wander over the endless volumes. Why did someone go to all the trouble of disguising the name of this library? What's hidden here? After awhile, Mr. Gardiner returns to her, looking sheepish. "Elizabeth, I'm sorry. Unfortunately, the old codger wasn't very helpful. He mumbled something along the lines of, 'If the gentry insist on playing detective,' and gave me this note. Now my business calls, so I'll meet up with you this evening." With these words, he departs, leaving behind a bemused Elizabeth. It seems somehow **out of line** that the librarian would put obstacles in her way—without even knowing her! . . . Seeing his grumpy face, she doesn't dare approach him **twice**. Instead, she examines the note more closely. What could this possibly mean?

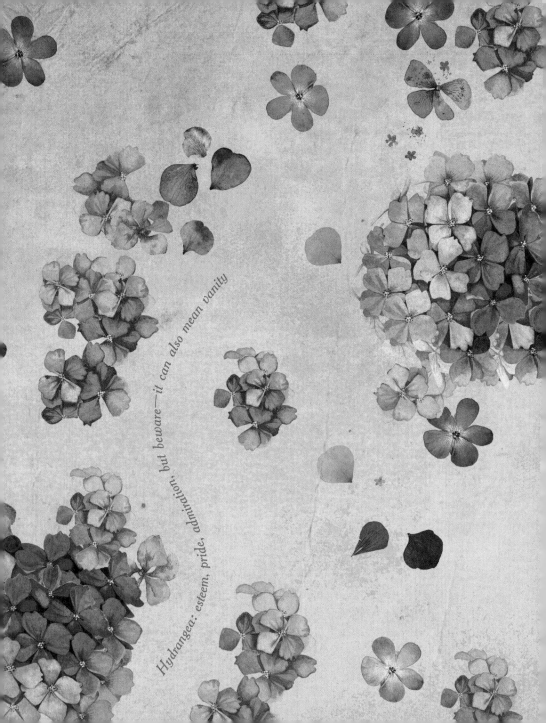

Hydrangea: esteem, pride, admiration, but beware—it can also mean vanity

Puzzle No. 6

White poppy: joy and vitality

The Seal

This must be the solution! After a brief look at the keyword catalog, Elizabeth hurries to the aisle indicated. And there it is, *Regency Etiquette: The Mirror of Graces*. Elizabeth eagerly removes the book from the shelf, opens it to a page with a bookmark, and reads, "Many people appear to be courteous, but, on closer examination, reveal that they are not . . ." When she looks more closely, she realizes that it isn't a bookmark—it's an envelope that was inserted near the front of the book. She inspects it more closely. There is neither sender nor recipient; there's only a seal on the back of the envelope. When she opens it, she discovers a thick stack of banknotes.

Is it conceivable that this considerable sum has something to do with her mysterious disappearance on that evening? And if so, who could be behind this wicked deed? Elizabeth examines the envelope closely. Didn't she see this emblem somewhere recently?

Wild rose: love,
tenderness, romance

Snapdragon: trust and the keeping of secrets

Bluebell: gratitude; "Our hearts beat as one."

Foxglove: "I've had bad experiences in the past."

Puzzle No. 7

White rose: innocence and devotion

White calla lily: immortality

Lily of the valley: deep love

Thistle: "The situation is too dangerous for me."

Mr. Collins

Of course! Elizabeth triumphantly raises up the envelope, causing the other visitors to the library to look her way. Rosings, it's the Rosings seal! She saw it just a few days ago at the ball! And before that—how often had Charlotte's husband, Mr. Collins, coerced her into visiting his neighbor, the Lady of Rosings, and she had sat there, longing for it to end, looking again and again at the clock that was decorated with this very emblem? Of course!

Lady Catherine de Bourgh has to be the most patronizing and overbearing person she's ever met! She appears to be devoted only to her nephew Mr. Darcy. She always refers to him in glowing terms, and when he came to dine, she treated him very graciously. So it should come as no surprise that, according to rumors, she wishes for her nephew to marry her daughter, thinks Elizabeth. Is it possible that Lady Catherine is behind this plot? Is she the one who schemed to ruin Elizabeth's reputation so that Mr. Darcy would lose interest in her and establish a connection with her daughter? What a horrendous idea! "Many people appear to be courteous, but, on closer examination, reveal that they are not . . ." Elizabeth lets out a bitter laugh. Evidently, Lady Catherine can't stand to have her will contradicted. But it's still inconceivable that such a supposedly fine lady would stoop to such nefarious means . . . pay someone money to involve her in a scandal. Was this the sole purpose of the ball? But whom could Lady Catherine have enlisted in her disgraceful endeavor?

Elizabeth thinks hard. She decides to consult her friend Charlotte once more about the affair. Not only was Charlotte present at the ball but also she knew and could assess Lady Catherine much better than Elizabeth, due to her proximity and frequent visits.

The next day, Elizabeth and her aunt return to Hunsford to visit the Collins family. Looking for Charlotte, Elizabeth runs right into the arms of Mr. Collins, who greets her wearing a grave expression.

"Fair cousin! I'm honored to be able to welcome you once again to my home after so short a time. Although recent events certainly won't reflect well on my reputation, I want you to know that I see it as my duty as your cousin to receive you in my house in spite of the untoward circumstances, although my ecclesiastical office obliges me to impart a few words of admonishment. As I learned from my highly esteemed patroness, Lady Catherine de Bourgh, who saw it as her moral duty to inform the rest of local society, you, dear cousin, disappeared from the ball of said patroness in the company of an unknown man. In addition, your destination is said to have been Gretna Green. I must say that I never expected such a wanton act from among the Bennet family." Hearing these words, Elizabeth first tries to compose herself and then answers, "If anyone has committed a wanton act, it is your much revered Lady Catherine." "I'm afraid I don't follow you, worthy cousin. Lady Catherine is a thoroughly honorable person of the noblest character who is not only blessed with great wisdom but is also known for her extreme kindness. I count myself supremely fortunate that she holds me in such regard. She recently turned to me for assistance in a matter that was extremely important and urgent, she said. Of all possible persons, she chose me to deliver a message of supreme importance, although I don't know any more details about the background or reasons behind it. But when my patroness entrusts me with a mission of such great significance, I cannot fail to fulfill her wish." Elizabeth goes over this in her head while Mr. Collins begins once again to sing the praises of Lady Catherine, of which Elizabeth had already had her fill long ago. Is it possible that her cousin was involved in this plot without his knowledge, all because of his loyalty to this dreadful person? As Elizabeth's mind intently and feverishly works on this idea, she catches only occasional words and phrases: ". . . I forget the name of the person I was supposed to contact . . . Was it something to do with a candle? . . . Something from a pig? . . . Oh, well, it doesn't matter; the task has already been carried out. Now, I must take my leave, fair cousin. Lady Catherine awaits."

Frustrated, Elizabeth remains behind. Mr. Collins is so scrupulous about the details, but he can't remember the key name! Maybe she can figure it out herself. Something from a pig . . . Curly-tail? . . . Pigs-ear? . . . Pork-knuckle? Didn't she recently hear about someone with a name like that? Elizabeth tries to think back. Obviously, the name is a compound of two parts; otherwise, Mr. Collins wouldn't have mentioned two things that are so incongruent . . .

Pink carnation: encouragement,

"I'll never forget you."

Red carnation: deep devotion, fascination; love

Red poppy: fertility; sleep; oblivion

Laudanum

...ees
...o for...
...ding 1893...
...Lion 2 0.1.0
for his Watch 0.4.0
...for Baer 0.1.0
26 cash 0.2.6
To go to Llandilo 0.1.9
mend his Watch 0.5.0
8 Baichel 0.1.0
...Wille 0.10.0
13 ham 4.0.0
To my Cloaths 0.10.0
21 cash 0.4.0
8 Cash 0.10.0
...ust 2 Mother 3.3.6
...ust 15 Cloaths 0.21.6
...tember 2 1.6.0
...Tall —

September 8
October 4
November 26
Dec. 24 to go to town
1895 January 2 Enoch
To go to Llandilo
Enoch Shops
Bur Mrs Pa...
Llandilo
...
March 27
April 1
...8
15

Orchid: appreciation for the beauty of the recipient

Plus: longing and passion

Puzzle No. 8

Common daisy: faithfulness, trust, purity, modesty

Soiree at the Bingleys'

Wick-ham—Mr. Wickham! Elizabeth can't believe it. Mr. Collins's fine patroness Lady Catherine really did offer someone money to ruin her reputation. And it was no less than the officer Mr. Wickham. So everything Mr. Darcy wrote in his letter about his former childhood friend was true. First, Mr. Wickham—after throwing away all the money that was legally his—made unjustified demands on Mr. Darcy and then planned to seduce his younger sister, Georgiana Darcy, so that he could obtain money by fraud and take his revenge on Mr. Darcy. Now, he had also agreed to involve her, Elizabeth, in a scandal for a fee. What a vile man! And her cousin Mr. Collins? This blowhard was surely the one to deliver the note that Charlotte found at the ball telling Mr. Wickham where he would find his payment. Well, well! The noble Lady Catherine was well aware of his reputation and wanted to make sure the deed was done before handing over the money. As she thinks about Lady Catherine, Elizabeth's face grows dark with rage.

She angrily relates all that she has learned to her friend Charlotte and her aunt. She would love to storm over to Rosings and confront Lady Catherine, but Charlotte wants to avoid a confrontation with her husband and her intimidating neighbor, and she tries to appease Elizabeth by suggesting that they instead try to restore her good name. "Dear Lizzy, I understand your inner turmoil. But what good would it do to confront Lady Catherine? The barn door was left open and the horse has bolted. Don't you think it would be more beneficial to do something to win back society's favor?" Elizabeth's aunt agrees. "She's right, dear. What's done is done." She tells her about an upcoming soiree at Netherfield to which Mr. Bingley has invited many distinguished guests. She promises that she'll try to obtain an invitation for Elizabeth, whose face now clears. Dear Mr. Bingley! Such a good-hearted gentleman—it's very possible that he would allow her to come to his soiree in spite of recent events.

When Elizabeth arrives at Netherfield with her mother a few days later, they're met with both curious and openly disdainful looks. Elizabeth gulps and decides to start by thanking her host for the invitation.

While she's speaking to Mr. Bingley, her gaze falls on Mr. Darcy's cousin Colonel Fitzwilliam. Mr. Bingley must have invited his friend's cousin, as well. The Earl and Countess and the Duke and Duchess are also in attendance. On the other side of the room, she sees Mr. Bingley's sisters, Caroline Bingley and Mrs. Hurst, who examine her with contempt and then whisper together. Elizabeth feels that she'll have to skirt all sorts of hidden obstacles that might trip her up on the way to restoring her reputation. Even though Miss Bingley and Mrs. Hurst are of high social standing, she'd be better off avoiding them this evening.

It appears that the two have no intention of allowing her to appear in a positive light but are determined to put her in an uncomfortable situation. At the same time, she fervently hopes that her mother knows how to behave and won't draw negative attention to herself through inappropriate actions. The last thing Elizabeth needs this evening when she's already under intense scrutiny is for her mother, in her tactless and clumsy way, to try to convince Mr. Bingley of the virtues of her daughter Jane. Oh, how Elizabeth wishes her sister Jane were here now! A friendly face would do her so much good.

Once again, Elizabeth lets her eye wander around the room. Who would be the best person to speak to? If she wants to improve her unfortunate situation, it would probably be best to speak to the highest-ranking guests. She takes a deep breath and makes her way through the room.

Anemone: expectation and hope, impermanence

Puzzle supplement
Titles of Nobility

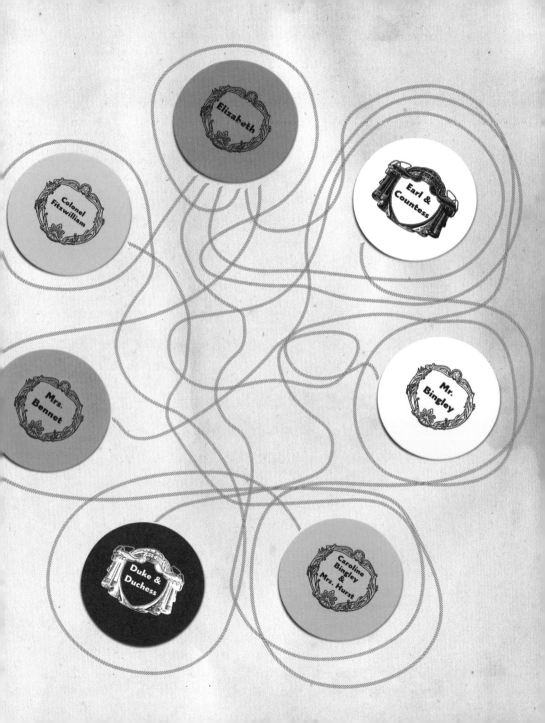

Ox-eye daisy: unadulterated happiness, genuineness

Daffodil: an unhappy love affair, gallantry, vanity

Puzzle No. 9

Geranium: *"I'll wait for you at the usual place!"*

The Bouquet

Elizabeth succeeds. She's standing before the highest-ranking guests among all those present. At the same moment, Colonel Fitzwilliam steps up and greets her warmly. He tells her how happy he is to see her again and then introduces her to the Duke and Duchess, with whom he is well acquainted. After they've conversed for a while, Mr. Darcy's cousin excuses himself and goes to discuss an important matter with one of the gentlemen present. Elizabeth is extremely impressed. The Duke and Duchess do indeed seem to be very open and friendly people, and after Colonel Fitzwilliam's departure, the three immediately engage in animated conversation. Because Elizabeth's manner is so open and sincere, the Duke in particular forms a positive impression of her and takes her aside briefly when the Duchess is addressed by another guest.

The Duke is planning a surprise for his wife, so he suggests that they retreat to another, somewhat quieter corner of the room. As Elizabeth follows the Duke, she passes very near to Colonel Fitzwilliam, who is engaged in deep conversation with another man.

"Miss Bennet, as I said before, my wife recently gave me the gift of a wonderful son, Lord Henry. In honor of the occasion, I would like to surprise her with a large bouquet of flowers, but, unfortunately, I'm no expert in the language of flowers. Our gardener told me that hydrangeas, ox-eye daisies, roses, and bluebottles are currently in full bloom in our gardens, as well as bluebells, calla lilies, carnations, common daisies, poppies, and gentian. My wife loves both noble and simple varieties. I know she's especially fond of daffodils and tulips and also likes lavender. Our gardener believes that white roses, hydrangeas, and white calla lilies make an especially lovely bouquet. Bluebells, white poppies, gentian, and ox-eye daisies also make a wonderful bouquet. Bluebottles, red poppies, yellow carnations, and common daisies look beautiful together. But he also told me that he's not familiar with the language of flowers. This may sound completely absurd for a man in my position, but I don't want to get myself into hot water. If you happen to have any knowledge in this area and could advise me, I would be extremely grateful."

Fortunately for him, this is very familiar territory for Elizabeth, thanks to a mother who wanted to make sure her daughter would know how to interpret any bouquets that she received. She smiles at the Duke. "You're in luck."

"Excellent!" he answers. "And would it also be possible to include one of her favorite flowers in the bouquet, do you think? That would make a truly marvelous summer bouquet."

Given Elizabeth's knowledge of the social significance and blooming period of the various flowers, what should she recommend for the bouquet?

Puzzle No. 10

The Sheet Music

In plain view of all those present, the Duke is thanking Elizabeth for her recommendation of bluebells, white poppies, ox-eye daisies, and gentian when they're joined by Caroline Bingley, who has been observing them together for some time. "Miss Bennet, what would you think of entertaining us on the pianoforte?" Turning to the Duke, she adds, "Your grace, I recently had the good fortune to hear her give a brief concert and enjoyed it very much." Elizabeth, who is well aware of the fact that she is not a superior pianist, replies, "You flatter me, but I wouldn't want to interrupt the lively conversations of the other guests with my playing." But Caroline Bingley won't take no for an answer and rejects her excuse. "I'd recommend 'The London March'! It's one of my favorite pieces . . ." Elizabeth, who can't refuse too vehemently in the Duke's presence, answers hesitantly, "Very well." As Caroline Bingley accompanies her to the pianoforte, Elizabeth tells her that it's been a long time since she's played the piece, so she's uncertain about how it starts. Caroline Bingley presses a book of music into her hands. When Elizabeth sits down at the piano and all eyes are on her, she realizes that the first two pages of the piece have been cut into pieces. She wants to speak to Caroline Bingley, but Caroline is already addressing the people gathered, calling for them to be silent and offering a few introductory words. Elizabeth knows that if she wants to maintain the good impression that she's managed to make on the guests so far, she must quickly reassemble the pages correctly.

Puzzle No. 11

The Newspaper Article

On her return from the soiree, Elizabeth is completely satisfied with the way the evening went. How nice the Duke and Duchess were! She's overjoyed that she was also able to give the Duke such helpful advice, for which he thanked her in front of everyone.

And how wonderful that Caroline Bingley didn't succeed in embarrassing her in front of the entire company. Although her playing wasn't perfect, she still received several appreciative and favorable comments.

The piece chosen by Mr. Bingley's scheming sister wasn't easy. Someone must have struggled with it before her; otherwise, why would they have written the governess's words on the sheets?

What did it say? "Don't drift off! Keep time!"

Elizabeth grins. Playing that piece at that speed, it certainly would be difficult to fall asleep. But she'll have no trouble falling asleep after her successful evening. It's been a long time since she has been this tired! She yawns loudly. But wait! Wasn't there a poppy pictured on the music? Suddenly, Elizabeth is wide awake. Yes, there was definitely a picture of a poppy on the music! "Drift off"—poppy—laudanum—laudatini—all of a sudden, it's crystal clear. The drink that she was given at the ball was made with laudanum. That's where the name "laudatini" came from. And that's why she can't remember how she ended up in the coach. Mr. Wickham must have supported her and dragged her to the coach. That's why it looked to the other guests as though she left the ball in his tight embrace . . .

Elizabeth feels the anger bubbling up inside her again and forces herself to look on the bright side. This evening was a resounding success. Would this delightful news spread as quickly as the scandalous gossip from a few days earlier? Elizabeth hopes so with all her heart.

When she opens the newspaper two days later, she gasps. She's once again the center of attention! Excited, she reads the short piece in the society column.

SENSATION!

After her recent scandalous disappearance from a ball with Gretna Green as her destination, Elizabeth Bennet has now made a brilliant social comeback. Who would have believed it? Following her misstep, Miss Bennet had plunged to second-to-last place on our list of marriageable young women for this year's ball season. In the middle of last week, she just managed to take 28th place away from Miss Thompson, whose popularity sunk even further when her extramarital pregnancy became known. In light of recent events, however, Miss Bennet has now been able to climb 15 places higher on our list. What a surprise!

Elizabeth snorts disdainfully as she reads. It's outrageous that they write about young women in this way! She feels deep sympathy for Miss Thompson and can easily empathize with her in her precarious situation. But at the same time, she's greatly relieved that her efforts have evidently paid off and she appears in the paper in a better light. So what position does she now occupy on the list?

Puzzle No. 12

The Needlework Sampler

Elizabeth is relieved. Thirteenth place! She seems to have once again found favor with society, and her reputation has been very much improved. How fortunate! And how splendid that Mr. Darcy's cousin Colonel Fitzwilliam was present at the soiree at Netherfield. So Mr. Darcy will also hear about the events of the evening from a reliable source. Certainly, Colonel Fitzwilliam won't paint a bad picture of her; he's very well disposed toward her, as far as she can tell from her visit to Hunsford. Nevertheless, she would be so glad if she could speak to Mr. Darcy in person in order to explain how she became mixed up in this scandal. Have his feelings for her changed?

After all the excitement, Elizabeth finally has a quiet moment to tell her favorite sister, Jane, about Mr. Darcy's letter and proposal. Elizabeth confesses that she's no longer indifferent to Mr. Darcy and that she would like to speak to him again. In an effort to help, Jane promises to think about it. "Don't worry, Lizzy. We'll find a solution; I'm certain of it."

The next few days pass rather quickly, and soon it's time for Jane's visit to her uncle and aunt in London, where she'll be spending several days. Unfortunately, Jane and Elizabeth haven't found an opportunity for a private conversation. Jane was besieged with requests from her younger sisters Kitty and Lydia to fetch all sorts of objects from London. Then she was pestered by her mother, who is certain that Mr. Bingley is still interested in Jane, even though he's not currently showing any signs of it. She's heard from Lady Lucas that he doesn't appear to be attached to anyone else. The entire neighborhood agrees.

As Jane is bidding Elizabeth farewell, she says, "There's something for you on your bed," and looks at Elizabeth with a meaningful glance. Curious, Elizabeth goes to see what it is. It's an alphabet embroidered by Jane, a needlework sampler, but incomplete. How strange; Jane's usually so conscientious! Elizabeth examines the letters and the embroidered ornaments closely and tries to organize her thoughts.

Puzzle No. 13

Afternoon Tea

A few days later, Elizabeth is on her way to Meryton to visit her aunt Mrs. Philips, who has invited her to tea, and Elizabeth is thinking about Jane's advice to invite Mr. Darcy and Mr. Bingley to dine. Jane is no doubt correct, but it's hardly an easy proposition. Her mother has made no secret of the fact that she finds Mr. Darcy to be too proud and condescending. Nevertheless, it's the ideal time for an invitation. She's heard that Mr. Darcy is once again staying with Mr. Bingley. It would be much easier to invite the two gentlemen together, while Mr. Darcy is in the neighborhood, than to do it when he's at his residence in London or at Pemberley.

When she sees her aunt's house, she sighs deeply. How pointless these tea parties are! But she doesn't want to disappoint her aunt, who would be sad if she declined at the last moment. Well, at least after the soiree at the Bingleys' and the newspaper article, she can hope that she'll no longer be the focus of gossip.

As she enters the room, she sees that her aunt is talking to two local women, Miss Watson and Mrs. Long, who are in the process of reporting on the latest news concerning the officers stationed in Meryton. After quickly greeting Elizabeth, they return to their important subject.

Mrs. Philips: "Did you hear that *Colonel Forster* and *Captain Carter* suddenly left the camp? I *thought* they were supposed to be stationed here!"

Miss Watson: "Yes, my *dear*, I heard the same thing. My *neighbor* told me about it. Apparently, there was an urgent matter, and they've been *transferred* up *north*. Although I only have it second*hand*, my neighbor has always *been* right about *these* things. She met them both before their *departure*. She told me this the day before yesterday when I *saw* her in Clarke's *library*."

Mrs. Long: "What a coincidence! I ran into *her* the *day* before yesterday just as she was coming out the *door*."

Once again, Elizabeth sighs deeply and sits down in a corner of the room. Her thoughts drift back to Mr. Darcy.

Miss Watson: "Yes, coincidences do happen! Such a *charming* and lovable person. But did you see the *dress* she was *wear*ing? Completely out of *fashion* . . ."

Mrs. Long: "The *muslin* fabric was very beautiful, but the cut . . ." She takes a sip from her teacup.

Mrs. Long: "By the way, the *tea* is excellent, my dear. And the *pastries* are also excellent!"

Mrs. Philips: "Thank you. I once ran into Mrs. Nicholls, the *Netherfield* housekeeper, at the *market*, and she told me that these are a favorite even among their highest-ranking guests."

Miss Watson: "Speaking of Netherfield, have you heard any *news* about that charming Mr. Bingley? I saw him this morning in his *curricle*, and he greeted me very *warmly*."

Mrs. Long: "I *learn*ed that, due to family obligations, he'll probably miss the start of this year's London ball season. But he wants to be present for the third *event*."

Miss Watson: "Oh, what a *shame*! That means that he'll be leaving very soon. I wonder whether he'll be *inviting* people to his *townhouse* again. The events he holds are doubtless always among the high points of the season, in my opinion. They say that he's currently being visited by a good friend, just a few days before his departure."

Mrs. Philips: "Yes, Mrs. Nicholls said that Mr. *Darcy* must have an important reason for his last-minute visit, but she couldn't be more *exact*. His coachman told her that an *axle* broke on his coach—you know, the big green one. Well, in any *case*, it's understandable that this situation would take *priority* because, as Mrs. Long said, the London ball season is about to begin. Unfortunately, there seem to be problems with the *repairs*, which is why the *coachman* appears to have his hands full."

Mrs. Long: "How annoying. Naturally, that kind of thing always happens at the worst *time*! My neighbor told me that recently, on the day before she *was* expecting important guests, one of her servants *slipped* and *dropped* the gravy bowl and its entire *contents* on the *dining room* carpet. Can you imagine? The whole *carpet ruined*?! How horrible! Of course, she was beside herself . . ."

On the way home, Elizabeth reviews the afternoon as she tries to sort through her thoughts and filter out the important parts of what was said from all the **trivialities.** Much of it can be **crossed out** mentally, but there was at least one important piece of information for her. Her thoughts wander **forward and backward** and **every which way.** What could it have been?

T	N	E	V	E	D	I	N	I	N	G	█	R	O	O	M	M	A	R	K	E	T
H	E	L	I	B	R	A	R	Y	D	L	N	E	█	E	S	R	I	A	P	E	R
A	S	S	H	A	M	E	A	C	E	E	O	T	S	L	I	P	P	E	D	T	O
N	U	T	H	E	S	E	E	R	P	N	S	S	N	C	T	I	M	E	E	H	B
D	O	O	R	W	A	S	L	A	P	O	A	R	A	I	T	E	█	H	A	E	H
T	H	O	U	G	H	T	E	D	O	L	E	O	M	R	P	C	P	E	R	E	G
I	N	V	I	T	I	N	G	R	R	O	S	F	H	R	A	A	A	R	L	S	I
N	W	C	A	R	T	E	R	█	D	C	D	L	C	U	S	E	H	X	A	A	E
I	O	O	F	N	O	I	H	S	A	F	A	L	A	C	T	T	A	█	E	C	N
A	T	D	E	P	A	R	T	U	R	E	Y	A	O	P	R	I	O	R	I	T	Y
T	D	E	R	R	E	F	S	N	A	R	T	B	C	O	I	█	T	R	A	T	S
P	C	H	A	R	M	I	N	G	E	█	C	O	N	T	E	N	T	S	W	E	N
A	D	E	N	I	U	R	S	A	W	A	R	M	L	Y	S	N	I	L	S	U	M
C	N	O	D	N	O	L	N	E	T	H	E	R	F	I	E	L	D	N	E	E	B

The most important information is:

Puzzle No. 14

The Dilemma of the Coach

Of course! The London ball season is about to start! That means that not only will Mr. Bingley have to leave soon but so will Mr. Darcy—and probably even before Mr. Bingley, if the words of those three women can be believed. Good gracious! And she had hoped to explain everything to him over a meal. How much time is there before Mr. Darcy leaves?

She thinks it through. The stagecoach takes half a day to reach London. It departs every day at 10:00 a.m. If Mr. Darcy selects this mode of transportation, he'll probably be leaving tomorrow morning because he won't want to have to meet his first social obligation on the day he arrives home. Traveling by private chaise or landau is certainly the most pleasant and most comfortable option. But because they're heavy coaches, they don't tend to reach such high speeds. Also, he needs to reckon with longer preparations before they're ready to travel. If he makes his final preparations today, he's likely to leave tomorrow morning. In a barouche, which is mainly used for jaunts and pleasure trips, it will take him a day to reach London. In that case, the departure time will have to be early tomorrow morning. With the light and sporty coach models, on the other hand, he could reach London in just a few hours, and no long preparations would be necessary. He wouldn't even need a coachman and would most likely depart late tomorrow afternoon.

But which mode of transportation is the most probable, given the unstable weather conditions expected over the next few days? Which coaches are available to him at Netherfield for his journey back to London?

Elizabeth tries to recall everything she knows about coaches, including all the details that she's picked up at various teas in her neighborhood and on her visit to Hunsford. Once again, she's attempting to sort out all the information in her mind.

If she'd known that these trivialities would someday become important and useful, she would have paid more attention! When can she expect Mr. Darcy to depart?

1. und 2.

3.

5.

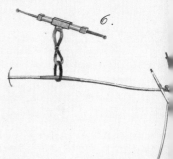

6.

	1. Stagecoach	2. Chaise (private)	3. Landau
Number of wheels	4	4	4
Number of draft animals (HP)	2–4	2–4	2–4
Coach box	Yes	Yes	Yes
Number of passengers	Depends on model	Depends on model	4 + 2 on the coach box
Driven by	Coachman	Coachman	Coachman
Roof	Fixed	Fixed	Folding top
Suitable for bad weather	Yes	Yes	Yes
	Public mode of transportation that members of the upper class would never use	Traditional chaise that's especially suitable for long journeys and bad weather	Luxurious and very expensive city carriage
	Public	Mr. Darcy, Mr. Bingley (currently being used by Caroline Bingley)	Mr. Darcy, Lady Catherine de Bourgh

4.

7.

4. *Barouche*	*5.* *Phaeton*	*6.* *Curricle*	*7.* *Gig*
4	4	2	2
2	2 (horses or ponies)	2	1
Yes	No	No	No
4 + 2 on the coach box	2 (+2 if there's a wooden bench for servants)	2	1–2
Coachman	Passenger	Passenger	Passenger
Semi-folding top	Partial cover	Partial folding top	Partial folding top
No	Partly	Partly	No
Expensive, prestigious second coach for good weather	Modern, sporty coach	Sporty and modern coach that young men like to drive at high speeds	Light and relatively inexpensive coach
Mr. Bingley	Lady Catherine de Bourgh, Mr. Darcy	Mr. Bingley	Mr. Collins, Mr. Bingley

Puzzle No. 15

Mr. Darcy's Goods and Chattels

Oh dear, Mr. Darcy is already leaving tomorrow toward the evening with
Mr. Bingley's curricle! How can she convince her mother to invite the two men at
such short notice? It isn't just that her mother has always disliked Mr. Darcy but
there's also barely time to prepare a formal meal that would befit their status or
to clean and arrange the house in preparation—two things that are normally very
important to Mrs. Bennet.

Nevertheless, Elizabeth has to try if she wants to be finished with this
dreadful affair.

When she speaks to her mother, the reaction is as expected. "But Elizabeth,
how could you even think of it? Is it really worth receiving Mr. Bingley with so
little preparation and serving him an inferior meal? Think of your sister Jane!
I believe she still hasn't given up hope that she'll be asked the most important
question of a woman's life. Is it worth alienating such an amiable and—more
importantly—wealthy man like Mr. Bingley for the sake of Mr. Darcy?"

Suddenly, Elizabeth has an idea of how she might persuade her mother.
Elizabeth herself would only enter into a marriage that was based on love and
equality. But for her mother, who's also looking out for her daughters' welfare and
income, the social position and wealth of the husband-to-be are key. Mr. Darcy is
said to have a very large fortune. "If you think Mr. Bingley is a wealthy man, then
you've never considered Mr. Darcy's riches."

Elizabeth tries to estimate the worth of Mr. Darcy's goods and chattels.

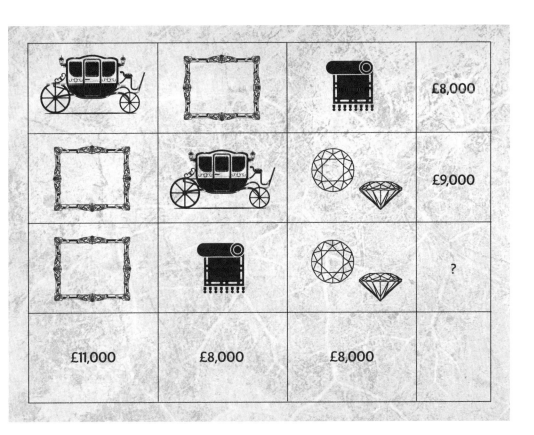

The value of the jewelry collection consisting of pieces inherited from his family comes to £_____; the sumptuous carpets are valued at £_____; his coaches are worth £_____; and his collection of paintings, including many valuable works of art, comes to £_____.

It's said that the value of his house in London is five times as much as the value of the jewelry and painting collection together. And his estate at Pemberley is worth twice as much as the London house.

This means that the total value of his assets is £_____.

Puzzle No. 16

The Preparations

When Mrs. Bennet hears that the total is £131,000, her enthusiasm knows no bounds. "How very rich and noble you'll be! What a lot of money you'll have for expensive jewelry and any number of carriages! Jane will have nothing by comparison—absolutely nothing! . . . Such a charming man! And how handsome he looks, so tall and distinguished! Oh, my dear Lizzy, forgive me for having considered him to be so disagreeable. Hopefully, he won't hold it against me." "Calm down, Mother. We're not yet married, nor are Jane and Mr. Bingley." "Yes, but given your brilliant reputation, it's just a matter of time! How exciting! Two married daughters . . ." She then adds, "Certainly, speed is of the essence. How I wish I had more servants! But don't worry. As Mrs. Darcy and Mrs. Bingley, you'll never again have to think about such things. What a wonderful day! First, I'll speak to Mrs. Hill and tell her to rush the preparations for tomorrow, then I'll take care of the invitation." "Thank you, Mother," says Elizabeth. But her mother is no longer listening. "Of course, the dining room and the sitting room have to be prepared. After having eaten, we'll surely have another cup of tea or coffee, or a game of whist in the drawing room; that's just common courtesy. But we can't forget the vestibule . . . And, of course, we need fresh flowers in the vases . . ." She leaves the room mumbling to herself.

When Mrs. Bennet speaks to Mrs. Hill, she learns that, with all the other preparations that have to be made, the servants Sally, Mrs. Hill, and Rose will only have 1½ hours tomorrow for cleaning the premises. Normally, Mrs. Hill cleans the vestibule surfaces in an hour. Sally is smaller and manages only ⅔ of what Mrs. Hill can do because her short stature means that she always needs a chair to reach the higher areas. Rose is especially nimble and achieves twice as much in an hour as Sally.

Mrs. Bennet wonders whether her three servants will manage to appropriately set up and clean the **relevant** rooms in time for the coming visit.

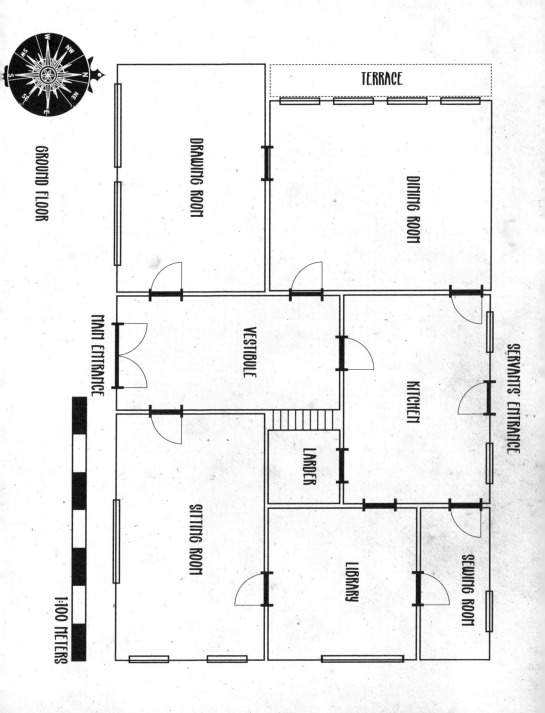

Puzzle No. 17

The Menu

The answer is no, but for Mrs. Bennet, the matter is settled. Postponing the meal and, in a sense, the weddings of her two daughters is out of the question. She searches feverishly for a solution. Finally, she decides to ask her sister in nearby Meryton for the quick loan of a servant to help her. Mrs. Philips is happy to comply, given the promising prospects.

The next day comes. Because all the servants are busy arranging and setting up the house for the upcoming visit, there's no time left over for running errands. After all the excitement, Mrs. Bennet feels compelled to take refuge in her room for a while out of consideration for her nerves. So it's up to Elizabeth to put together a meal worthy of her noble guests using the foods available in the larder and garden, as noted in the list that the servants hastily drew up beforehand. Before Mrs. Bennet retreats to her room, she tells Elizabeth that she wants to make a good impression on her guests, so there will be no cold dishes served. Not only that, but she is also of the opinion that a person like Mr. Darcy with such a high annual income will most probably not be satisfied with only one meat dish.

Elizabeth looks at the list and then gazes out the window at the rear courtyard, where the chickens are happily clucking away as they wander about. Fortunately, the weekly meat delivery comes today, and the neighbor has already brought them the day's milk ration. Of course, this will mean that they'll have to do without meat for the rest of the week, but she's sure that her family won't mind. What sort of menu can she put together using the available ingredients? She would like to serve at least three dishes.

Pan-Fried Oysters with a Butter Sauce and Chestnuts

Take two pounds of the largest oysters you can find, open them, remove the meat, and drain them in a fine-mesh strainer, setting aside the oyster water.

Rinse the oysters in hot water. Prepare a batter: Beat two egg yolks and grate in half of a whole nutmeg. Cut up a little lemon peel, combine it with a large amount of parsley, a spoonful of spinach juice, and two spoonfuls of cream or milk, and stir flour into the mixture until it becomes a thick batter. Have a pan ready with a little butter and dip the oysters in the batter one at a time.

Dredge the oysters in breadcrumbs and fry them until brown. Remove them from the pan and keep them warm.

Peel and skin two pounds of chestnuts, fry them in butter, and remove them from the pan. Pour out the grease and sprinkle a little flour in the pan. Place a piece of butter the size of a hen's egg in the pan and slide it around with a spoon until the butter has melted and you have a creamy mixture. Now add the oyster water and three or four mace blades and stir in several shelled and add the chestnuts, one cup of white wine, and a mixture pistachios. Simmer the mixture for a little while and then of two egg yolks and four tablespoons of cream. When the sauce has thickened, transfer the oysters to a bowl and pour the sauce over the top.

Garnish with chestnuts and lemon.

Recipes

Breast of Lamb in a Bread and Herb Crust:

— Boil two breasts of lamb until the ends of the bones extend out of the water and the meat can easily be detached from the ribs and skin

— Brush meat with the yolk of one egg

— Sprinkle with a few chopped herbs (marjoram, hyssop, tarragon, and parsley), chopped onion, breadcrumbs, salt, and pepper

— Brown lightly in a casserole dish

— Make a gravy from the meat juice and serve

Chicken Fricassee

or Sauce for Roast Veal

For this recipe, you'll need two chickens that have already been skinned and cut into small pieces. Rinse the meat in hot water and pat it dry with a cloth. Boil the meat in a pot with milk and water until it's tender. In a clean pot, heat a cup of cream and a quarter pound of butter. Stir until the butter has melted and then continue stirring to prevent the fat from separating.

Using a fork, place the chicken pieces in the pot with the butter and cream. Add several mace blades, finely ground nutmeg, and a few mushrooms and simmer for two to three minutes before serving the chicken fricassee.

If you don't have mushrooms, you can add a spoonful of chopped gherkin to give the dish a fine acidity.

This sauce is also ideal for roast veal and is delicious with rice.

RICE PUDDING

Place a quarter pound of rice in a pot with a cup of cold milk and a pinch of cinnamon and bring to a boil.

Stir occasionally so that the rice doesn't stick to the bottom of the pot.

When the rice is done, transfer it to a pan. Add a quarter pound of cold butter and sugar to taste. Then grate half of a whole nutmeg and add it to the rice along with three or four spoonfuls of rosewater and stir well.

When the rice has cooled, separate eight eggs. Beat together the yolks and half the whites and stir them into the rice.

Grease a mold, fill it with the rice, and bake. You can also roll out puff pastry dough beforehand and place it over the milk rice.

Or you can add a few raisins and dried fruits.

Summery Pea Soup:

- Peel a cucumber, cut it lengthwise into quarters, and then into slices
- In a deep casserole dish, combine the cucumber slices with the chopped, light-colored inner leaves from two heads of romaine lettuce, two handfuls of mint leaves, two thinly sliced onions, a little pepper, a little salt, a pound of young peas, some chopped parsley, and half a pound of butter
- Cook gently for at least 1½ hours until the vegetables are tender
- Meanwhile, boil a pound of wrinkled peas until tender, drain in a colander, and combine them with a portion of the cooking liquid (amount depends on how thick you want your soup)
- Mix thoroughly with the rest of the soup and serve hot.

Chicken with Plum Stuffing:

- Bring half a pound of dried plums to a boil in a little water, remove them from the heat, and let them stand for fifteen minutes
- Cut two slices of white bread into cubes and brown slightly
- Combine the white bread, chopped herbs (parsley, thyme, marjoram, and sage), a tablespoon of apple cider vinegar, a tablespoon of sugar, and the finely chopped plums. Use this mixture to stuff the chicken and place it in a pot
- Mince the offal (minus the liver)
- Add one onion cut into quarters, one onion studded with two whole cloves, two celery stalks cut in half, one bay leaf, half a bunch of parsley, three thyme sprigs, three tablespoons of malt vinegar, and the offal to the pot along with just enough water to cover the chicken
- Bring to a boil, then cover and simmer for 1½ hours
- Melt a tablespoon of butter and stir in one to two tablespoons of flour to form a paste

- Continue stirring while gradually adding 2/3 cup of milk. Measure out a cup of chicken broth and add
- Continue simmering and stirring until the sauce becomes velvety
- In a second pot, heat 2/3 cup of cream with the peel and juice from one lemon, then stir this mixture into the sauce and season with salt and pepper
- Let the chicken cool completely (preferably overnight)
- Heat the sauce until it becomes spreadable and brush it onto the entire chicken. Serve with thin slices from one lemon, parsley, and several dried plums

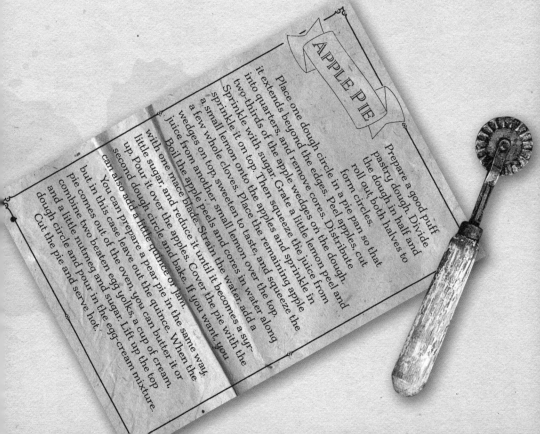

APPLE PIE

Prepare a good puff pastry dough. Divide the dough in half and roll out both halves to form circles.

Place one dough circle in a pie pan so that it extends beyond the edges. Peel apples, cut into quarters, and remove cores. Distribute two-thirds of the apple wedges on the dough. Grate a little lemon peel and sprinkle it on top. Then squeeze the juice from a small lemon onto the apples and sprinkle with sugar. Place the remaining apple wedges on top, sweeten to taste, and squeeze the juice from another small lemon over the top. Sprinkle a few whole cloves on top, add a little sugar, and reduce it until it becomes a syrup. Strain the pie with the juice from one mace blade. Cover the water, add a little quince or jam. If you want, you up. Pour it over the apples and bake. Boil the pie in the same way, second dough circle and a pear pie in the quince. When the can also prepare a little butter it or

You can leave out the quince. When the pie comes out of the oven, you can butter it or but in this case two beaten egg yolks, a cup of cream, combine a little nutmeg and sugar. Lift up the top and a little pour in the egg-cream mixture. dough circle and serve hot. Cut the pie and

Irish Lamb Stew:
- Cut a lamb shoulder into six steaks, dust with flour, and brown lightly on both sides
- In a stew pan, melt two tablespoons of butter, then add two tablespoons of flour and heat slowly until the mixture turns light-brown
- Gradually add meat stock or broth and bring to a simmer
- Add the steaks, three small chopped rutabagas, and two finely chopped carrots. Cover and simmer gently for one hour
- Season to taste with salt, pepper, and two tablespoons of mushroom ketchup
- If the sauce is too fatty, stir a little flour into cold water, then stir this into the pan and return the stew to a boil

Braised Rump Steak with Potatoes
- Pound eight rump steaks with a meat mallet and season with salt and pepper
- Slice four tablespoons of butter and distribute the pieces in the bottom of a saucepan. Place a layer of meat on the butter and cover with a layer of cooked, sliced potatoes
- Repeat these layers until the saucepan is almost full, then fill with stock
- Cover and simmer for three hours until the meat is tender
- Drain the liquid into a pot, skim off the fat, and thicken it with a little butter and flour. Pour this mixture over the steaks
- Return them to a boil and season with salt

List of Supplies

1 pound dried plums
2 handfuls raisins
White bread
3½ pounds rice
1 small bottle apple cider vinegar
1 small bottle malt vinegar
1 pound sugar
10 pounds flour
5 onions
1 basket mushrooms
2 pounds potatoes
1 pound butter
1 pound smoked ham
1 handful whole cloves
1 bay leaf
Mace blades
Finely ground nutmeg
Cinnamon
Salt
Pepper
2 lemons

4 pints milk
1 pint cream (skimmed off yesterday's milk)

7 eggs

2 stalks celery
10 carrots
2 artichokes
3 zucchini
2 cucumbers
2 heads romaine lettuce
1 pound young peas
1 pound wrinkled peas
Parsley
Thyme
Marjoram
Hyssop
Tarragon
Sage
Mint

Thursday meat delivery: 2 breasts of lamb

1 Pint = 2 cups

1 Pound = 16 ounces

Puzzle No. 18

A Place in Society

Once Elizabeth has solved the problem of the menu and has chosen to serve Summery Pea Soup, Chicken Fricassee, and Breast of Lamb in a Bread and Herb Crust, she's faced with her next challenge. She has to find a suitable seating arrangement that takes into account her family's sensitivities, habits, and preferences. And, of course, she wants her guests, Mr. Bingley and Mr. Darcy, to feel comfortable. But the most important thing is to sit next to Mr. Darcy so that she can talk to him quietly and explain how she ended up in this scandalous situation. A difficult task!

She thinks it through. As the head of the family, her father, Mr. Bennet, must, of course, sit at the head of the table. Her mother, Mrs. Bennet, will want to sit to the right of her husband to spare her nerves after all the excitement of the past few weeks. At the same time, Mrs. Bennet will definitely want to discuss the latest news about the officers with her daughter Lydia. It would also be a good idea to seat Mrs. Bennet far from Mr. Darcy and out of his line of sight, since she hasn't always made the best of impressions and another compromising situation should be avoided at all costs. She's sure her sister Kitty will want to sit next to Lydia— the two are practically inseparable! However, Kitty won't want to sit next to or across from Mr. Darcy because he always intimidates her. And it's best if Lydia is also seated far from Mr. Darcy. Her simplemindedness combined with her fondness for the latest gossip and tittle-tattle about the officers wouldn't be conducive to Mr. Darcy forgetting about the incident with Mr. Wickham. But if Elizabeth knows Lydia, her sister won't have any interest in the two guests, Mr. Bingley and Mr. Darcy. Thanks to Mary's equanimity, she can be seated anywhere. Elizabeth would like to be seated near Jane, as her closest confidante. At the same time, it would certainly be helpful if Elizabeth's amiable sister were seated in the middle to serve as a buffer between the guests and the family members, given their sometimes dubious behavior. Of course, the meal will also serve as an opportunity to effect a rapprochement between Jane and Mr. Bingley, provided they're able to sit next to one another and converse quietly. Elizabeth so badly wants this for her sister! Mr. Bingley seems to be a truly fine and likable man. As a close friend of Mr. Darcy's, they should also be seated near one another.

Elizabeth reexamines her seating plan. It simply has to work! Hopefully, she'll finally be able to have a quiet talk with Mr. Darcy and win back his affection.

Happy Ending

A Second Chance

Nervous but determined, Elizabeth takes her place at the table next to Mr. Darcy. She glances uncertainly toward the other end of the table, where spirits are high, no doubt due to the imminent and unexpected return of Colonel Forster and Captain Carter. Mr. Darcy seems unimpressed. After a few clichéd greetings, Elizabeth listens as Mr. Bingley plucks up his courage and—almost bashfully— tells Jane of his devotion.

Elizabeth sees how her sister's face blushes but then becomes radiant. Elizabeth can't help smiling and winds up her own courage. She starts to explain to Mr. Darcy how the scandal came about. He waits until she has finished speaking to respond: "I have to confess, I wanted to seek you out much sooner. From the very start, I harbored doubts about the story I'd heard, and when my cousin Colonel Fitzwilliam wrote about meeting you at Netherfield, I took that as an opportunity to immediately visit my friend Mr. Bingley. Unfortunately, my coach suffered a broken axle on the way, and its repair has turned out to be more difficult and time-consuming than I expected. That's why I couldn't come to you in person." Elizabeth answers with relief: "Yes, I heard about that." Mr. Darcy continues, "If you'll allow me, I also have a lot to tell you, but maybe the two of us could talk alone over a cup of tea in the drawing room or sitting room?" Elizabeth smiles and stands. "There's nothing I would rather do."

The Surprise Of The Year!
Two Grand Betrothals At Netherfield And Pemberley!

It was recently announced that Mr. Fitzwilliam Darcy has become engaged to Miss Elizabeth Bennet. At the same time, Mr. Charles Bingley became engaged to Miss Bennet's sister Miss Jane Bennet.

This is indeed great cause for celebration!

RECENTLY PUBLISHED BOOKS

WONDERFUL SCOTLAND: A travelogue with 20 fine engravings that include scenes of Loch Lomond, LOCH NESS, and the untamed beauty of the Isle of Skye. By James Robertson.

Box No. 1

PATHS THROUGH THE PRIMEVAL FOREST. Happiness is the SOUTH! With this travel guide by L.A. Byrinth, you'll reach your destination WITHOUT detours or OBSTACLES—for a carefree travel experience.

Box No. 2

BALLET, The Royal Opera House—Announcement. Last week, the famous Russian prima ballerina Anna Lebedeva arrived in London, where she plans to give a number of performances with her ensemble. Despite the fact that she barely speaks English, she has no problem communicating because, according to her philosophy, DANCE speaks a thousand WORDS because dance LINKS us. She's looking forward to the upcoming events. Tickets are available immediately from the usual outlets.

Box No. 3.1

PETERSON'S PATENTED LAMP is so bright, nothing will ever get by you again. Thanks to the candleholder's ingenious technology, it optimally reflects the LIGHT of a low-soot wax candle and illuminates every corner.

Box No. 3.2

TO IMPROVE CONCENTRATION—The following tricks are thought to improve one's power of concentration: Recite the ALPHABET forward and backward, or JUMP from one end of the alphabet to the other and back again, or recite tongue-twisters. Nothing helps? Try our new remedy, "Ginkgophile," made from the extract of gingko plants. Sold by all purveyors of medicines.

Box No. 4

The British Museum Library announces: **SEEKING** capable **LIBRARIAN** who works SYSTEMATICALLY, sees the bigger picture by looking RIGHT and left, and is well versed in both literature and numbers.

Box No. 5

RECENTLY PUBLISHED BOOKS

THOMAS KITCHIN'S NEW UNIVERSAL ATLA With a completely revised MAP of the United Kingdom of Great Britain and Ireland RIGHT AT THE START. 28 detailed maps with all the RELEVANT INFORMATION.

Box No. 6

THE BIG BOOK OF NAMES. By E. Hill. Examines origins of ENGLISH NAMES. Whereas "Mills" and "Smith" are clearly derived from a specific profession or refer to a geographical feature, the origins of other names are not so cl and even seem to be RANDOM COMBINATIONS. But o even these names follow a pattern. An extremely interesting book that clarifies backgrounds and establishes new links.

Box No. 7

FAUX PAS
Anyone who frequents society should first learn the customs of the country. At yesterday's reception, the Prussian envoy committed the faux pas of greeting the Earl first and then t Duke, despite the fact that the two gentlemen were standing side by side. Apparently, the DUKE was willing to overlook envoy's misstep and bid him a warm welcome.

Box No. 8

Change of location: The local authorities would like to announce that the **FLOWER MARKET** is moving to Columbia Road, effective immediately. Market traders who wish to peddle their BLUEBELLS, OX-EYE DAISIES, an GENTIANS are asked in future to set up their stands near fountain at the corner of Garden Street.

Box No. 9

RECENTLY PUBLISHED BOOKS

Do you sometimes feel lost? Be guided by THE WRITTE WORD. It can help you to navigate seemingly hopeless situations and can provide support. Expanded and revised edition of **THE BOOK OF COMMON PRAYER.**

Box No. 10

ULY 5, 1813.

)TICE from the **BOOKMAKER:** Anyone who placed a
on Arrow yesterday can now collect their winnings. The Earl's
se, a popular favorite, remained lodged in 13th place until
last moment when he was overtaken by Conley, who then
IZED 13th PLACE. Disappointingly, Pegasus came in last.
Box No. 11

**HAT'S MISSING IS OFTEN WHAT'S MOST
IPORTANT.** Respectful treatment of you and your
eavement. We help you cope with the loss of a loved one by
king after all the details and SORTING OUT the estate.
ite Rose Morticians, Graham Street 18.
Box No. 12.1

RECENTLY PUBLISHED BOOKS

R JOHNSON'S HANDBOOK OF GRAMMAR.
2 volumes. Volume 1: SMALL STAYS SMALL. Among
er things, provides a comprehensive explanation of how to
attributive adjectives in elliptical constructions, as well as
inite and indefinite articles and superlatives. Volume 2: BIG
AYS BIG. Provides explanations of how to form compound
ins, when to insert a hyphen, etc.
Box No. 12.2

SS TAYLOR WOULD LIKE TO ANNOUNCE:
customers who are obliged to economize, the dressmaker
gests that they SEEK OUT SEPARATE items of clothing
: are OUT OF FASHION, reuse PARTS of outfits, or
ance them by COMBINING them with new elements. She
ld also like to inform the public that she has just received a
ment of the finest French lace.
Box No. 13

PASSIBLE ROADS
raordinary rainfall and strong gusts of wind over the past
days have taken their toll and made numerous roads im-
sable. At least two incidents were reported in which coaches
ered a BROKEN AXLE, one of which was the LANDAU
well-to-do gentleman, witnesses said. Because the weather
cast for the next few days indicates that more rainfall is
ible but by no means a certainty, we can expect that the
s will soon be usable once again.
Box No. 14

RECENTLY PUBLISHED BOOKS

BASIC MATHEMATICS. By G.H. Hardy. Basic mathematical knowledge such as how to solve an equation with a
variable and an explanation of MATHEMATICAL OPERA-
TIONS that is easy to understand. Price 8 s, bound.
Box No. 15

Young, hardworking woman offers her **SERVICES AS
HOUSEHOLD HELP.** This industrious woman, who
previously demonstrated her excellent skills in the house of
her uncle, is a capable cook, cleaner (24 square meters PER
HOUR), and runner of all sorts of errands. If interested, please
send inquiries to **R.M.** at A.M., Davies Street 14.
Box No. 16

SUCCESSFUL OPENING
The opening of the exhibition by up-and-coming artist
H. Granville was a resounding success. But the exhibited
works weren't the only attraction. Many visitors also enjoyed
the musical accompaniment provided by the string quartet, as
well as the culinary offerings. A large number of select COLD
DISHES were served, such as CHICKEN WITH PLUM
STUFFING and roast beef, along with a selection of fine
wines. When asked, all visitors to the exhibit agreed that the
artist has a bright future ahead of him. His works can now
be viewed daily at Grand Street 10.
Box No. 17

A woman with a vast wealth of experience gleaned from many
years of service as a **GOVERNESS OFFERS HER
SERVICES.** Special attention given to forming the mind
and manners, among other things. For example, she teaches her
young pupils that when they are seated at the table, they should
speak only to their immediate neighbors or persons SEATED
OPPOSITE THEM. Conversing with guests seated farther
away is not done by proper young ladies who don't wish to raise
their voices at the table. Room and board to be provided, fees
negotiable. Send inquiries to Mr. Blackwell, Kensington Road,
addressed to J.E.
Box No. 18

Solutions

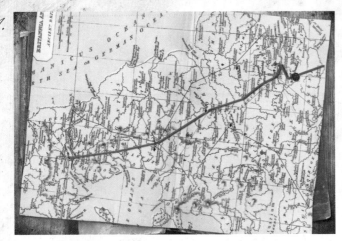

1.

Elizabeth is traveling along the blue route.

2.

13.

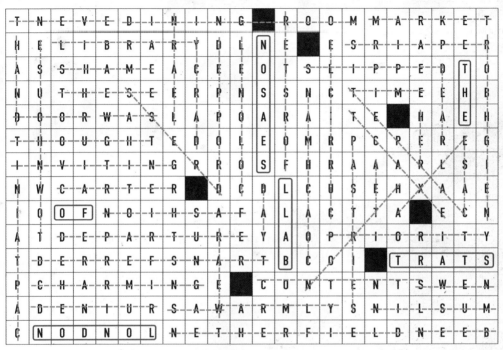

14. Mr. Darcy returns to London in Mr. Bingley's curricle because the landau that he arrived in is not yet roadworthy. Mr. Bingley's other available coaches are definitely unsuitable for bad weather. So Mr. Darcy leaves the next day toward the evening.

Solutions

15. Coaches: £1,000

    Painting collection: £5,000

    Carpets: £2,000

    Jewelry collection: £3,000

    Third row of the table: £10,000

    House in London: £40,000

    Pemberley: £80,000

    Total estimated assets: £131,000

16. In one hour, Mrs. Hill normally cleans 18 square meters, Sally 12 square meters, and Rose 24 square meters. Together, they clean 81 square meters in 1½ hours. They have to clean a total area of 98 square meters. This means that they won't be able to clean the necessary rooms within the time allotted.

17. Elizabeth can serve Mr. Darcy and Mr. Bingley Summery Pea Soup and, as hot meat dishes, Chicken Fricassee and Breast of Lamb in a Bread and Herb Crust. Because they raise their own chickens, she has all the ingredients she needs.

18. The seating arrangement is as follows:

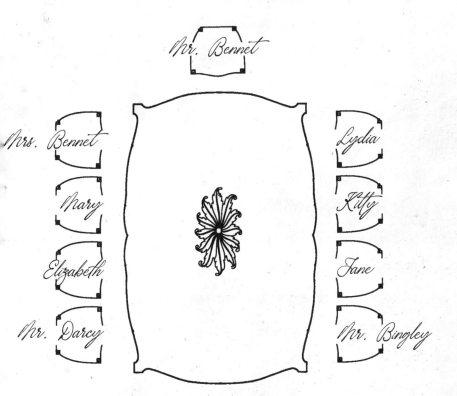

Mr. Bennet

Mrs. Bennet   Lydia

Mary   Kitty

Elizabeth   Jane

Mr. Darcy   Mr. Bingley

Solutions

Game Accessories

Notes:

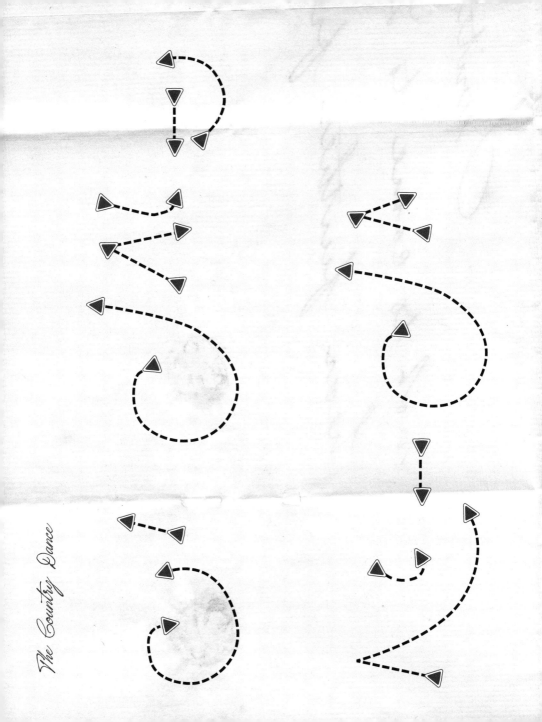

The Country Dance

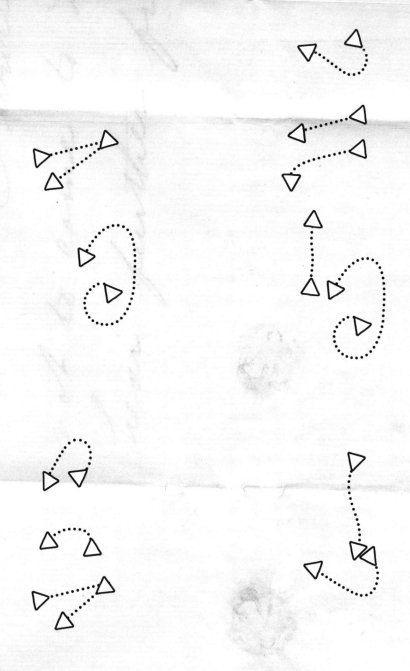

Titles of Nobility
Peerage

British nobility is conferred by the king or queen.
A distinction is made between peerage and gentry.
One difference is that peers have a right to a seat in the
British Parliament's House of Lords for their allocated region.
Peers generally also hold additional, lower-ranking titles.
The eldest son holds the next-highest title until he inherits his father's title.
The nobleman's wife holds the female counterpart to his title.
Daughters of Dukes, Marquesses, and Earls are addressed as Lady.
Daughters of Viscounts and Barons are addressed as The Honorable.

Wife: The [Marchioness (of)] [name of territory]
Eldest son: **Marquess (of)** [name of territory]
or **Lord** [name of territory]
Younger sons: **Lord** [first name] [last name]
Daughters: **Lady** [first name] [last name]

Marquess
(of) [name of territory]

Wife: The **Marchioness (of)** [name of territory]
Eldest son: **Earl (of)** [name of territory]
or **Lord** [name of territory]
Younger sons: **Lord** [first name] [last name]
Daughters: **Lady** [first name] [last name]

Wife: The **Countess (of)** [name of territory]
Eldest son: **Viscount (of)** [name of territory]
Younger sons: **The Honorable** [first name] [last name]
Daughters: **Lady** [first name] [last name]

Viscount
(of) [name of territory]

Baron
(of) [name of territory].

Wife: **The Viscountess (of)** [name of territory]
Sons: **The Honorable** [first name] [last name]
Daughters: **The Honorable** [first name] [last name]

Wife: **The Lady (of)** [name of territory]
Sons: **The Honorable** [first name] [last name]
Daughters: **The Honorable** [first name] [last name]

The titles of nobility held by the gentry are **Knight** and **Baronet**.
Both titles are granted by the royal house as a special distinction and are not
associated with land ownership, rights to a territory, or a seat in Parliament.
Unlike **Knight**, the title of **Baronet** can be inherited by an eldest son.